More
Bible
Baddies

BOB HARTMAN

Illustrations by Jeff Anderson

LION
Children's Books

Text copyright © 2001 Bob Hartman
Illustrations copyright © 2001 Jeff Anderson
This edition copyright © 2001 Lion Publishing

The moral rights of the author and illustrator
have been asserted

Published by
Lion Publishing plc
Sandy Lane West, Oxford, England
www.lion-publishing.co.uk
ISBN 0 7459 4421 3

First edition 2001
10 9 8 7 6 5 4 3 2 1 0

A catalogue record for this book is available
from the British Library

Typeset in 11.5/14 Baskerville BT
Printed and bound in Great Britain by
Cox & Wyman Ltd, Reading

Contents

Introduction

Why another book of Bible baddies? The answer is simple—the Bible is full of them! There are reasonably famous baddies like Judas and Goliath, who somehow got squeezed out of the first book. Then there are the more obscure baddies, like Ananias and Simon Magus, whose stories are fascinating and demand to be told. And, finally, there are the 'ladies'! Yes, that's right. For some reason (and I can't remember why), there were no women baddies in the first book. I thought that was just a bit unfair, so I have included three women here—Jezebel, Sapphira and one of my all-time favourite Bible baddies, Athaliah, the evil granny!

Some people have told me that the stories in this book are darker than the tales in *Bible Baddies*. And I think that's true. We are dealing with some serious badness here, after all. But I like to think that I have included some lighter moments, as well. Light in the humorous sense—particularly in the case of the two villanous couples. And light in that other sense, too—as in the sudden light which sometimes comes to people and makes them change their lives for the better.

This book is dedicated to the memory of my grandmother, who not only told me the story of the aforementioned evil granny, but also helped to introduce me to the light. She's been gone a long time, but I've never forgotten her stories. I hope that some of the tales in this book will be as memorable.

Bob Hartman

The Tempter's Tale
(part 1)

▪ ▪ ▪ ▪ ▪ ▪ ▪ ▪ ▪ ▪ ▪ ▪ ▪ ▪ ▪

THE STORY OF ADAM AND EVE

I t's strange, really. The moment we make a wrong choice—
the second we buy into badness—it all seems so clear.

'It's just this once,' we say to ourselves. 'No one will get
hurt. It doesn't really matter.' And on and on the excuses go.

But later, when we look back at what we've done—
when we have to deal with the shame or the guilt or the
consequences—the choice doesn't seem so clear. And, so often,
we wonder how we could ever have made such a foolish
decision in the first place.

That's certainly how it goes in the story you are about to
read—the story of where badness begins. But you may not feel
an overwhelming sense of the presence of evil. No, what you
will feel instead, I think, is a lingering sense of sadness and

regret. And that is as it should be. Because, in a way, this story is also about where badness leaves us in the end.

He hacked at the ground with his rough stone axe. He hacked at the weeds and at the bushes. He hacked till the sweat poured off his forehead and the calluses rose on his palms. He hacked until he could hear his heart pounding in his ears. But still the slithering thing slipped and squirmed away. So he sank down onto a stump and waited for his breath to return and his heart to stop racing. He wiped the sweat from his brow and stared at his hands. And that's when it all came back—the crushing memory of 'before', the pain of the paradise he'd lost.

It was like a bad bruise. It hurt to touch it, but touching it reminded him that it was there. Sometimes a smell would trigger it. Sometimes it would wake him in the night. Today, it was simply the sight of his hands.

Knuckles gnarled and cracked. Palms rough and swollen. Veins running down the backs like tree limbs.

'Were these the hands,' he wondered, 'that once tended a Garden? The hands that stroked the lion's mane and traced the zebra's stripes and danced across the rhino's wrinkled hide as he gave each one its name? Were these really the hands of Adam?'

Sometimes it seemed impossible. Sometimes it seemed too good to have been true. And sometimes he wondered, how had it happened? How had he let it all slip between those rough and dirty fingers?

As if to answer the question, a voice called from across the rocky field.

Yes, he had blamed her once. Blamed her more than once. But he knew now that the fault was his, as well as hers.

Eve called again, and then walked slowly towards him. It was almost impossible to see her as she had once been. The years, and the children, and the endless toil it took just to survive had erased for ever the woman who had danced happily in the Garden.

He shut his eyes. He shut them tight. He shoved his fists into the sockets and for a second, just a second, there she was again. Flesh of his flesh. Bone of his bone. At the dawn of their life together. He remembered touching her hair. And her lips. And tracing the shape of her face with his fingertips. And he remembered the prayer he had prayed. 'Thank you, Creator,' he had said, 'for this face and for this morning, and for all the mornings to come.'

'Adam!' the voice called again. 'Adam, why are you sitting there? Get back to work! We have a family to feed!'

Adam winced. There was still a trace of that other Eve in her voice. The same voice that had called out so many years ago called out across the Garden, 'Adam, come quickly! There is someone I want you to meet!'

That voice was so sweet. The face so innocent and gentle. She skipped towards him, excited like a foal or a fawn. She took his hand (he could feel those fingers, still). And she led him, laughing, to the Knowledge Tree.

There was no reason to be alarmed. No cause for concern. Those words had no meaning then. All was trust and goodness and love. How could he have known?

How could either of them have guessed that their new acquaintance would teach them the meaning of those words—and many more awful still.

The Serpent was a handsome creature. Confident. Persuasive. Poised. There was venom in his words but, at the time, his arguments seemed reasonable.

'So the Creator forbids you to eat from the Knowledge

Tree?' the Serpent had asked. 'He says that if you do, you will die? Well, what does he have to hide? That's what I want to know. And if he truly loves you, why would he want to keep anything from you? I suspect that he's afraid—afraid that if you eat from the tree, then you will know as much as he does! So why don't you taste the fruit and find out for yourselves?'

Even now, even after all the pain and the toil and the years away from the Garden, there was a part of Adam that still wasn't sure. Perhaps the Serpent was right—perhaps the Creator was just jealous of what he knew and did not want to share it. Was it so wrong to want to know? To know evil as well as good?

Adam looked up. His wife was staring at him, and the answer was there, in the lines on her face and in the sadness that never left her eyes. No amount of knowledge could make up for what those eyes had seen: their forced exile from the Garden, the angel with the fiery sword who was there to make sure they could never return, the desolate land they were condemned to till, the murder of one son by another...

Adam looked away and shook his head. His children had often asked him—what did the fruit taste like? Sweet like an apple? Sour like a lemon? How could he have told them the truth? Told them without seeming a fool? That it smelled of decay. That every bite was rotten. That it tasted like death. Death and regret.

Adam pounded his fists against his temples—as he had pounded them a thousand times before.

What if? What if? What if?

What if they had ignored the Serpent? What if they had obeyed the Creator?

What if they had never tasted the fruit?

Would he still be wrestling the lion and running with the

zebra? Would he still wake up each morning in the soft wet grass and trace his finger across Eve's forever beautiful face?

The thought was simply too much to bear. And so he picked up his axe again and began to hack at the earth. Eve grunted her approval and turned to walk away. But once she was out of sight, he listened again for the hissing one.

The Creator had made a promise—Adam remembered. The handsome one, the confident, persuasive creature, would lose his limbs and crawl upon the ground. And one day—surely he was remembering this right—one day, Eve would bear a child who would crush that serpent's head!

But who was this child? And where was this child? All Adam could do was hope. Hope that the Creator's promise would come true. Hope that someone would someday destroy the Serpent. Hope and keep on hacking. Hacking at the ground. Hacking at the bushes. Hacking at the weeds. Because hacking was easier than yearning for what might have been. Because it was better than longing for the life he lost when he left his beautiful Garden.

The Tempter's Tale

(part 2)

● ● ● ● ● ● ● ● ● ● ● ● ● ●

THE STORY OF JESUS IN
THE WILDERNESS

My son is a fan of martial arts films—all that high-kicking kung-fu fighting stuff! And in every one of those films, right at the end, there is always the Big Confrontation between the good guy and the bad guy. But before that—usually quite early on in the film—there is another battle, a smaller battle, where the good guy and the bad guy discover each other's strengths and weaknesses. That's the battle I've chosen to deal with in this story. Not the Big Confrontation between Jesus and the devil—the one at the end of the story where the devil's triumph on the cross is snatched away three days later. The one where he is left holding nothing but an empty tomb. No, this is

the earlier battle, the quiet one in the desert, where they looked at each other face to face and tested each other's strength and will.

You may notice similarities to Adam's story. That's because the Bible sometimes calls Jesus the 'Second Adam', come to fight the enemy that Adam could not beat.

He scratched at the ground with his cracked, dry fingers. He scratched at the dirt and the pebbles and the sand. He scratched out shapes and circles and lines. He was doodling. He was thinking. He was praying. He was hungry!

For forty days he had fasted. Forty days without food. Forty days in the desert. Forty days alone. Forty days to chart the course his life would take. Forty days to consider what it meant to be the Saviour of the world!

Fasting clears the head, he had been taught. Fasting helps you to see things more clearly. Fasting brings you closer to God. And all these things had proved true. But fasting also makes you sick with hunger—aching, gnawing, belly-screaming hunger! And maybe that is why he was suddenly no longer alone.

His companion was handsome. Confident. Persuasive. Poised. And his suggestions seemed not only sensible, but kind.

'If you're hungry, why not eat?

'If you're the Saviour of the world, why not use your power?

'If there are stones, why not turn them into bread?'

Jesus considered the words—considered them carefully. And he considered the face of his companion. The smile could not have been more genuine, the eyes more sincere. But the words—the words were lies. The words were filled with poison.

'There are more important things than bread,' Jesus replied. 'That's what the scriptures say. There is God, and all that he wants to give us. So if doing without bread helps me to get closer to him, then I am quite happy to go hungry for a while.'

'The scriptures,' his companion nodded. 'Of course. There is a great deal of truth in them, isn't there? Just the other day, I read this remarkable passage about the angels. Shall I tell you about it?'

Jesus just shrugged. He suspected that it would have been pointless to say no. He had it on good authority that his companion was nothing if not persistent.

He sat down beside Jesus and scratched some lines of his own in the sand.

'Imagine this,' he said, tracing out a perfect sketch of a tall and majestic building. 'The Temple in Jerusalem. Do you see it? And here, at the top of the very tallest tower, someone who wants attention. Someone who needs to gather a crowd. Someone who wants to demonstrate God's power. Someone like you, perhaps.'

He sketched a tiny figure at the top of the tower, and then drew a long line down to the ground below.

'Now suppose this someone was to leap from the Temple top. Do you know what the scriptures say would happen? The scriptures say that if that someone was Someone Special—God's own Son, perhaps—then the angels would come to his rescue before his feet ever touched the ground!'

Jesus nodded and traced out the shape of a heart. 'Yes, they do. But the scriptures also say that God loves us, and that we should trust that love. And that it would be wrong to put ourselves in foolish and dangerous places simply to put that love to the test.'

'But what about your mission?' asked the companion, more confident than ever. 'Surely saving the world is your life's work. And if it's the world you want, then I am the one to give it to you.'

He stood up. He waved wide his arms. And a hot wind swept up a desert's full of drawings. Armies and palaces. Treasures and thrones. All that anyone could ever want sprang up before Jesus and stood glittering and gold against the purple sundown sky. And all the while, his companion's words kept echoing in his ears.

'All of this will I give you if you will bow down and worship me!'

But Jesus did not move. For there were other words, as well. Words that he knew from his childhood and before. And these were the words he whispered as he drew one last shape on the ground.

'I will worship the Lord my God and him alone will I serve.'

Jesus looked up. The vision was gone, and so was the smile on his companion's face.

'I don't understand,' he said. 'I offer you the world and you draw an X through it?'

'Not an X,' said Jesus. 'A cross.' And that is when he noticed the blood on his companion's head.

'You're hurt,' said Jesus.

'It's nothing,' muttered his companion.

But as they stared at each other, both of them remembered one more scripture—a promise, an old promise, about a child and a battle and a crushing blow to a serpent's head.

'I will be back,' said the companion.

'I will be waiting,' said Jesus.

And suddenly he was alone again. Considering the course of his life. Thinking. Praying. Doodling. So he scratched at the ground with his cracked dry finger—scratched a circle beside the cross. The shape of the sun as it set? The whole of the moon as it rose? Or the mouth of an empty tomb?

The Trickster's Tale

. . . .

THE STORY OF JACOB

'You reap what you sow.'

'The bad things you do come back to haunt you.'

Whatever image you choose—gardening or ghost—the story of Jacob looks, at first, like proving these sayings true.

Jacob deceives both his brother and his father to win an inheritance. And, in turn, he is deceived—first by his uncle and then by his own sons. It looks as if the story has come full circle, and Jacob has got what he deserves. The trickster is tricked. The End.

But that's not actually how it goes. Because somewhere along the line, Jacob runs into God. And even though their relationship turns into a bit of a wrestling match, Jacob discovers that God is far less interested in punishment than he is in mercy and forgiveness. So while Jacob still reaps some of *what he sowed and still has to deal with the odd haunting dream, he also finds something else. He finds a new strength and renewed faith in God. And that's what makes his story so compelling.*

Jacob held the coat against his face, and rocked gently back and forth. His tears mixed with the bloody stain. The ragged rips in the cloth tore holes in his heart. His son, Joseph, was dead—bloody and torn like the coat, consumed by some savage beast.

There was nothing that could comfort him. No words to wail that would make any difference. There was just a hole where his son had been—a hole that would never be patched or mended.

Jacob had other sons, of course. But Joseph was special, the child of his beloved Rachel. He could hear them talking and laughing outside the tent. Jacob was no fool. He knew they hated their brother—hated him because Joseph had known he was special and had not let them forget it. But that was no excuse. The dead—even the despised dead—deserve respect.

Jacob tried to sleep. He folded Joseph's torn coat—the coat he himself had made—and tucked it under his head for a pillow. Then he shut his eyes and prayed that sleep would come and take his pain away.

But all sleep brought was dreams. And the dreams were more painful still.

Soon Jacob was dreaming about brothers. Not the noisy young men outside, but Jacob himself and his twin brother Esau. His mind whirled back to life at home as a young man...

They had always been rivals. Esau, with his red locks, hairy arms and strong back, was their father Isaac's favourite.

And Jacob, smaller and rather fragile, was ever under the watchful eye of their mother Rebekah.

At last the time came for Esau to claim his birthright. He was the elder of the two, just, so tradition dictated that blind old Isaac's blessing should be given to him—along with the right to rule the family and inherit the family fortune!

But Rebekah was canny and clever and shrewd, and she was determined that her favourite, Jacob, would receive that blessing instead.

And so the dream went on, as Rebekah's voice echoed around inside Jacob's head.

'Take your father his favourite meal.

'Lower your voice. You'll sound just like Esau.

'Wrap your arms in these goat skins. Your father's blind, but he's no fool. He'll want proof.

'And when he is convinced that you *are* your older brother, that is when you should ask him for his blessing!'

The dream was so clear, so real. Jacob saw himself in the dream smiling a smug smile, delighted. For the trick had worked! And, once given, the blessing could not be taken back!

And he saw his brother, Esau, beside himself with anger. His face matched the colour of his bright red hair. Esau knew there was nothing he could do about what had happened. But he was ready to kill the brother who had tricked him and stolen his birthright, and Jacob knew it.

Jacob woke with a start. He wiped the sweat from his face and rolled over. His sons were still talking and laughing. And as sleep washed over him and the dreams returned, he wished that they would be quiet. He wished that they would just go away.

'Go away!' his mother was telling him. 'Go away as far as

you can. Go to my brother, Laban.'

Jacob went, and discovered that his mother's deceitfulness was something that ran in the family.

Jacob's uncle, Laban, had two daughters. And Jacob fell in love with the youngest almost at once.

Jacob stirred in his sleep as painful images from the past came into his mind...

'Work for me for seven years,' Uncle Laban was telling him, 'and pretty Rachel will be your wife.'

So Jacob worked. It was long, hard, honest labour. But when the wedding day arrived, he was shocked to find a different daughter by his side.

'Leah's the oldest,' Uncle Laban grinned, neglecting to mention that she was by far the plainest, as well! 'It's only fair that she should marry first. But I suppose if you worked, say, another seven years for me, you could marry Rachel, too.'

Jacob had been tricked! Jacob was livid. And it was only now, seeing himself in his dream, that he was able to recognize the same expression that had been on his brother Esau's face.

Trickery or not, Jacob was determined to win Rachel. And seeing as there were no other ugly daughters hanging about, he thought that he stood a decent chance this time. So, in order to marry the girl he truly loved, Jacob worked for another seven years.

Jacob was tossing and turning now and he shivered as his dreams brought back more memories...

Now Jacob was a grown man with wives and a family and servants and flocks of his own. More than anything, he wanted to go back home. But would Esau still want revenge? Would Jacob's life still be in danger? He did not know the answer to those questions. All he could do was return and hope.

When he had reached the borders of his brother's land, Jacob sent his servants ahead of him.

'Take the sheep and the cattle with you,' he told them. 'And if you should meet Esau, tell him that they are a gift from his brother Jacob—a brother who longs to be reunited with him.'

Next, Jacob sent his family—as an expression of his trust and goodwill. So now he was to spend one night alone, at the side of the River Jabbok—a night that would change his life for ever.

It might have been a dream itself, so strange was the experience. But as he watched it all again, Jacob knew that it had been real…

His attacker came from nowhere—out of the dark and the night. He grabbed Jacob round the waist and threw him to the ground. Jacob tore himself free from his attacker and turned to face him. He expected to see a thief, or a madman, maybe. Or perhaps, even, his brother, Esau. But Jacob's attacker was none of those. He was bigger and stronger than any man that Jacob had ever seen. And there was something about him that had made Jacob wonder if he was even human!

Jacob knew he should run away, but there was something inside him that needed to go on wrestling. He had been wrestling all his life, it seemed. Wrestling with his father and his brother and his uncle, Laban. Wrestling to hold on to what he believed was his. And so he held on to his attacker, as well—they wrestled all through the night!

'Who are you?' Jacob cried. 'What do you want?' But his attacker did not answer him. They grunted and struggled and rolled on the ground. And even when the attacker put Jacob's hip out of joint, Jacob did not let go. Finally, as the sun began to rise, Jacob's opponent spoke.

'Let me go!' he said. 'The day is upon us.'

'No!' Jacob answered, struggling for breath. 'I will not let you go unless you give me something.'

'All right, then,' the opponent agreed. 'You will no longer be called Jacob—I will give you a new name. From now on you shall be known as "Israel" for, as the name suggests, you have struggled with God and persisted to the end!'

'Struggled with God?' Jacob wondered. 'But that must mean…' And so he asked. He had to ask. 'Then what is your name?'

Jacob's opponent smiled and said, 'I think you already know the answer to that question.'

And then he was gone!

Jacob fell to the ground and rubbed his aching hip. 'Could it be?' he wondered. 'Could it really be that he had seen the face of God, wrestled with the Almighty—and lived?' And suddenly, everything made sense—the whole of his long, wrestling life. God had a purpose for him. The struggles were all for a reason. To shape him and make him into the man, then the family, then the nation that God had promised to his father, Isaac, and his grandfather, Abraham.

And so Jacob rose and limped across the river, made peace with his brother Esau and returned to the land of promise. It looked as if everything would turn out all right.

But now… now Jacob's dream had become a nightmare. For Joseph, his special son, was dead. And all the struggling and wrestling had been for nothing.

Meanwhile, outside the tent, two of Jacob's other sons listened to him stirring and groaning.

'He's not taking it well,' one son observed.

'What did you expect?' shrugged the other. 'Joseph was his favourite.'

'Perhaps we should have told him the truth—that Joseph was sold into slavery.'

'What? And admit that we were the ones who did the selling? I don't think so, and besides, it's all quite fitting, if you ask me. The old man got up to his fair share of tricks when he was our age. Now the last laugh is on him.'

It wasn't, of course, for the God who wrestled with Jacob had one more trick up his God-sized sleeve. Joseph was on his way to Egypt. And when he arrived, God would help him rise to the top of the kingdom, where he would one day save his family and be united with them again.

But that's another story. About another dreamer. And another set of dreams!

The Bully's Tale

• • • • • • • • • • •

THE STORY OF GOLIATH

The story of David and Goliath is probably one of the best known in the Old Testament.

It's not hard to understand why. The world is full of bullies.

When I was seven years old, my family moved house and—wouldn't you know it—there was a bully living right across the street! I was short and shy and chubby—perfect bully fodder. And I was beaten up regularly.

In those days, parents had but one response to that kind of situation—'Stand up for yourself, boy! Fight back!'

So, one day, that's exactly what I did. It was hard and it was scary, but I clenched my fists and waved my arms, and the bully ran away!

I was amazed. I was in shock. In fact I was so confused

that the only thing I could think of doing was to knock on the bully's back door and apologize to his mother (did I mention that I was also excruciatingly polite?).

I'm not sure what I learned from that experience at the time, but I can tell you what I think now.

The bigger we get, the bigger the bullies get, too. So sometimes, somebody (and maybe even the last person you would expect) has to stand up and do something hard and scary. Somebody like Martin Luther King, who dreamed of a day when all people would be treated equally, regardless of their race. Somebody like William Wilberforce, who spent a lifetime arguing that slavery was wrong. Somebody like Mother Teresa, who argued that all people—poor people and sick people and people who were still waiting to be born— deserved our protection and care. And—who knows—maybe someday, even somebody like you!

He hated little things. And maybe that was because he had never really been little himself.

He'd been a baby once, of course. But he was the biggest baby the people of Gath had ever seen! So it was big robes and big sandals and big toys, right from the start. And, 'Don't push that little boy, dear.' And, 'Careful with that pot, child.' And, 'Don't squeeze the kitty so hard, Goliath—you'll hurt him.'

Little things. Little kitties. Little people. The world was full of them! And it didn't take long for them to notice that he was different—and to bring it, constantly, to his attention.

Some children return teasing with humour. Others with sullen stares. But Goliath chose fear. Even the most harmless comment about his size would result in a furious beating from the big boy. Yes, he was beaten up a few times, himself—by some of Gath's older lads. But he soon outgrew them all, and then no one dared challenge the boy who stood nearly seven feet tall!

'There's only one thing to do with bullies...' his father finally said. 'The army! That'll sort him out.'

Given his size and his strength, he might have risen high in the ranks. But his obvious hatred for the 'little generals' and their 'little rules' kept him marching with the infantry. In the end, there was only one thing Goliath was good for— frightening the enemy. And he was very good at that indeed!

He'd strap on his armour—all 125 gleaming pounds of it.

Then he'd pick up his spear—ten feet long, with a ten-pound iron point.

And finally he would stand at the front of the Philistine troops—a shining monster of a man.

'A challenge!' he would roar—and his roar rumbled across the valley to whichever army was camped on the other side. 'A challenge is what I offer! Send your best man to fight me. And if he wins,' and here Goliath always had a little chuckle, 'we shall be your slaves.'

A few men had taken up his challenge. Little men. With little swords. Goliath always smiled when he remembered how he had crushed their little heads and left their little bodies broken and twisted and torn.

Most men, however, never even tried. His presence alone made their little hearts beat with fear and sent them retreating to their little tents.

He expected as much today. The Israelites were not just a little people, they were the littlest of them all! A few scattered tribes. A puny, ramshackle army. And if what he had heard was true, they had just one little god to protect

them. It hardly seemed worth the trouble, but he marched out anyway into the valley of Elah and issued his customary challenge. He anticipated a short day's work. But he had no idea how short it would turn out to be.

The Israelites heard the challenge, as they had every day for the past forty days. And, to a man, they trembled. But someone else heard the challenge, too. Someone who had never heard it before. And it made him angry.

Maybe it had to do with his feelings about his people. Maybe it had to do with his feelings about his God. Or maybe he was just tired of being little.

David was the youngest of eight brothers, after all. And no matter how much courage he had shown, defending his father's flock of sheep, they all still thought of him as the 'runt'. Hand-me-down sandals and pass-me-down robes— that was his lot. And while his older brothers were able to serve as soldiers, the best he could do was to bring them lunch and carry chunks of goat's cheese to their commanders!

'If only,' David dreamed, 'I could do something big, for a change.'

And then he heard Goliath's challenge.

'So what do you get if you beat the giant?' he asked a soldier close by.

'A king's ransom,' the soldier answered. 'And the king's own daughter.'

'Well,' mused David, 'I'm surprised someone hasn't accepted the challenge already.'

And that's when he felt a hand—a big hand—on his shoulder. The hand belonged to his oldest brother, Eliab.

'What are you doing here?' Eliab growled.

'Bread… umm, cheese…' David muttered.

'Excuses, more like it,' Eliab growled again. 'Get back to the fields, where you belong!'

But David did not go back to the fields. No, he crept along the front lines, talking to one soldier after another, always about the giant. Finally, word got back to King Saul, who asked to see the boy.

The giant meanwhile was still waiting.

'Their little hearts are in their little throats,' he chuckled, in a nasty sort of way. Then he looked down at his shield-bearer. The little man was not chuckling back. In fact, it was all he could do, in the hot noonday sun, to keep himself and the shield standing upright.

'Pathetic,' Goliath muttered, and then wondered if the Israelites would ever send him a challenger.

'So you want to fight the giant?' grinned King Saul.

David had seen that look before. He got it from his big brothers all the time. It was that 'I'm-not-taking-you-seriously-you're-just-a-little-shepherd-boy' kind of look.

So David stood as tall as he could and answered with the straightest face and the deepest voice he could manage.

'Yes, Your Majesty, I do.'

'And what makes you think you can beat him?' the king continued, more seriously now.

David didn't even have to think.

'I have fought lions,' he said. 'And I have fought bears. All to save my father's sheep. And every time, the Lord God has helped me win. I am sure he will do the same with this giant.'

The king didn't know what to do. The boy had courage. The boy had faith. But if he allowed him to fight the giant, the boy would also soon be dead! Still, he needed a champion—any champion! So he made the boy an offer.

'My armour,' said the king, pointing to the other side of the tent. 'At least take my armour. My shield. My sword. My breastplate. Whatever you like! You will need all the protection you can get.'

David looked at the armour. He even tried a piece or two of it on. But it was much too big and much too heavy for him.

'I have all the protection I need,' he said to the king, at last. 'The Lord God himself will be my breastplate. He alone will be my shield.' And he bowed and turned and walked out of the tent.

Goliath, meanwhile, was tapping one big foot on the ground and humming an old Philistine folk song.

'In another minute, we're going back to camp,' he said to his shield-bearer, who breathed a relieved sigh and thanked every god he could think of. But before he could finish his prayer, a cheer rang out from the Israelite camp. Someone was walking onto the battlefield.

'At last!' Goliath drooled, like a hungry man who has just been told it's dinnertime.

The figure looked small, at first. Goliath put it down to the distance. But the closer he got, the smaller it seemed, until the giant realized, at last, that his challenger was no more than a boy!

'Is this some kind of joke?' he muttered to his shield-bearer. But neither the shield-bearer nor the boy was laughing.

'Or is it...' and here the giant's words turned into a snarl, 'is it some kind of Israelite insult? Do they mock me? Do they make fun of me? Well, we'll see who has the last laugh!'

And then he roared—roared so the ground shook, and the shield-bearer, as well.

'Do you think I am a dog?' he roared. 'That you come at me with this little stick of a boy? Send me a real challenger. Or surrender!'

'I am the real challenger,' said David, in that deep voice

he had used before the king. 'And the God I serve is the real God. He will give me the victory today!'

Goliath had heard enough. He grabbed his shield and raised his spear and charged. Little people and little generals and little soldiers. Little things had plagued him all his life! And now this little boy and his little army and his pathetic little god were going to pay. He'd skewer the lad and crush his little head and show everyone what someone big and strong could do!

But as he rushed towards the boy, David calmly reached into his shepherd's pouch. He placed a small stone into his sling and he swung it round his head. Then he prayed that God would make his throw both strong and true.

The stone and the giant sped towards each other. And at the last moment, Goliath caught a glimpse of it—a tiny speck, a minute fragment, so small it was hardly worth avoiding. But when it struck him between the eyes, he roared and he cried and fell crashing to the ground. And that little thing was the last thing that the giant ever saw!

The Rotten Rulers' Tale

• • • • • • • • • • • • •

THE STORY OF AHAB AND JEZEBEL

I've often wondered—do baddies really think they're bad? Did Hitler or Stalin ever say to himself, 'I'm responsible for the deaths of millions of people. I must be a real monster!'

Somehow, I doubt it. I reckon that even the baddest of baddies do what the rest of us so often do—they justify the wrong things they have done and then just get on with their lives.

But what if there were baddies who knew exactly who they were? And even found a certain wicked pleasure in their deeds? That's the idea I've tried to explore in this story—with two of the 'baddest' baddies of them all, Ahab and Jezebel.

36
• • • • •

King Ahab wanted to be wicked. He wanted it in the worst kind of way! But he lacked the courage. And he lacked the imagination. And worst of all, he lacked the will—the 'killer instinct' that true wickedness demands.

His queen, Jezebel, however, lacked nothing. She was, without question, the most wicked woman he had ever met. And this just made things worse. For, given her expertise at evil, her artistic flair for foul play, he could never hope to impress her with any wickedness of his own.

She sensed this, of course (even the most wicked have their compassionate side), and tried her best to cheer him up.

'Who's the wicked one, then?' she would ask playfully, over breakfast.

And Ahab would blush and lower his eyes and answer coyly, 'You don't mean me, do you, darling?'

'Of course I do!' she would coo. 'Who betrayed his own people? Who put my god, Baal, in place of Yahweh, the God of Israel? Who murdered Yahweh's prophets? And who chased his true believers into hiding? It was you, my dear— that's who. Wicked King Ahab!'

'Well, I couldn't have done it alone,' he would mutter in a humble sort of way. 'I had a wonderfully wicked wife to help me.'

'Nonsense!' Jezebel would reply coyly. 'You're quite wonderfully wicked all on your own!'

Then the conversation would turn to the weather (dry, always dry!), or to the state of the economy (failing crops, starving cattle), and ultimately to that pesky prophet Elijah, who had somehow managed to stop the rains from falling.

'If I ever get hold of him,' Ahab would rant, 'I'll murder him!'

'I'll do more than that!' Jezebel would reply. 'I'll torture him—slowly—and stand there and laugh as he dies!'

'I'll rip off his fingers!' Ahab would return.

'I'll tear out his hair!' Jezebel would shriek.

And on and on it would go, until the two of them would collapse in fits of evil laughter. It was, on the whole, a strange sort of relationship. But it seemed to work for them.

One morning, however, King Ahab failed to appear at the breakfast table. And when Jezebel found him—on his bed, in his room—he had a woefully unwicked expression on his face.

'What's the matter, dear?' Jezebel chirped. 'Run out of prophets to kill?'

'No,' Ahab sighed. 'Something much worse than that. It's the vineyard, next door.'

'Naboth's vineyard?' queried Jezebel. 'What could possibly be the problem with Naboth's vineyard?'

'It's in the way!' Ahab moaned. 'That's the problem! My little garden is much too small. I want to put in some cabbages, next year. And some sprouts. And two more rows of those little potatoes you like so well. But his stupid vineyard is right smack up against our wall. I've offered to buy it. I'd give him more than what it's worth. But the selfish so-and-so refuses to sell! So what can I do?'

Jezebel tried hard to hide her frustration. There were plenty of things that Ahab could do. He was king, after all! And a wicked king (or a wicked wannabe!), as well.

The answer was obvious. But would telling him, straight out, snuff out the spark of true villainy she had worked so hard to ignite? Would it fracture his already brittle evil self-esteem? In the end, she decided to take matters into her own hands.

'Leave it to me,' she said quietly. Then she turned the conversation to the weather.

Later that day, while Ahab was out digging in the garden,

Jezebel sneaked into his chambers and picked up his pen. She wrote letters to all the elders and noblemen in Naboth's home town. She forged Ahab's signature (she'd had plenty of practice—so it was perfect!). And she marked each letter with Ahab's special seal.

My dear friend and servant,

I have a favour to ask of you. Would you proclaim a day of fasting—a special, holy day—in your town? Would you be so kind as to invite my neighbour, Naboth, to this event (he has a lovely vineyard, don't you think?)? Please give him the most prominent seat at the event—a place where everyone can see him? And then would you hire two villains (I have names and references) to stand up in the middle of the ceremony and accuse Naboth of some heinous crime? Blasphemy against his god, perhaps. And disloyalty to the king. And then, and I hope this is not asking too much, would you drag Naboth from that place and stone him to death?

Thank you very much for your consideration. I do hope that this will not be too much of an inconvenience. As always, my concern is for your continued health and well-being, which will be assured by your prompt response to this request.

Regards,

Ahab, king of Israel

Jezebel cackled and clapped her hands. There was a joy to pure evil that never failed to delight her. Naboth would die (she had never liked the look of his vineyard anyway!). Ahab would get his plot of land. And the local noblemen would be convinced, once and for all, of her husband's utter and total wickedness. She couldn't wait to see the look on his face.

Her wait lasted only a few days. Ahab appeared at breakfast, one morning—a changed man.

'I'll have two eggs for breakfast, this morning,' he grinned. 'And—why not, by Baal!—a few rashers of bacon, as well!'

'So what's got into you?' asked Jezebel innocently.

'Haven't you heard, my dear?' Ahab beamed. 'Naboth is dead. His widow wants to sell. And now, at last, his vineyard will be mine!'

'How wonderful!' said the queen. 'So tell me—how did poor Naboth die?'

'It was most unusual.' Ahab mumbled through a mouthful of egg. 'Blasphemy. Treason. Not very neighbourly, if you ask me. But then the rumour is that the charges were trumped-up. As if...' and here the king's chewing became more deliberate, 'as if someone truly wicked had it in for him.' And here he stared at his queen.

Jezebel could contain herself no longer. She blushed and she nodded, like a schoolgirl caught with a love note.

'Yes, my darling, I was the one who arranged it. I thought, at first, that it might be better to leave it to you— wicked man that you are. But you were so miserable! And in the end, I just wanted to see you happy again.'

Ahab held up his hand. 'Enough,' he said, solemnly. There were tears in his eyes, and little yellowy bits of egg on his trembling lips. 'I have been blessed with the most exquisitely evil wife in the whole world. What more could a wicked king ask for?'

And then he gave Jezebel a big, sloppy, eggy kiss. It was, on the whole, a disgusting thing. But it seemed to work for them.

Ahab's celebration was short-lived, however. For, as he strolled through his new vineyard later that day, he was surprised by an unexpected guest.

'Elijah!' Ahab cried. 'What are you doing here?'

The king's voice was shaking. Shaking with anger, as he remembered the threats he had made against this man. And shaking with fear, as well—for this was the man who had stopped the rain.

'I have a message for you from my God,' Elijah solemnly replied. 'The God who sent a drought upon this land. The God who was once your God, too.

'The Lord says, "You have murdered poor Naboth, and now you want to steal his property, as well! I promise you this: on the very spot where the dogs lapped up the blood of Naboth, they shall lap up your blood, too." '

Ahab's shaking was all fear now. 'Naboth... no... you don't understand.' He tried to explain. 'Jezebel... it was all her doing.'

' "And as for your wife, Jezebel," the prophet continued, "the dogs will do even more. They will chew her to pieces and leave so little behind that even her dearest friends will not be able to recognize her!" '

Ahab wanted to be wicked. He really did. He wanted to turn his evil threats into reality. He wanted to rip off Elijah's fingers and tear out Elijah's hair and torture Elijah and murder him. But it's hard to be wicked—really hard—when what you actually feel like doing is running away!

Ahab was scared—more scared than he had ever been in his whole sorry life. So he ran from the vineyard and hid in his room and wept and wailed and hoped that Jezebel wouldn't notice.

The noise was hard to miss, however, and Jezebel was humiliated by her husband's behaviour—a feeling that turned to disgust when he told her his battle plans over breakfast, one morning.

'It looks as if we'll have to fight the Syrians,' he said thoughtfully, as he lifted a dripping spoonful of porridge to his mouth. 'And the prophets have told me that I will die in the battle.'

'Not Elijah, again!' Jezebel groaned. 'If I hear the story about the dogs one more time…'

'No, no! Not just Elijah,' Ahab interrupted. 'But the prophet Micaiah, as well.' And Ahab dropped the spoon back into the bowl. 'But here's the thing,' he went on. 'I think I have outsmarted them with a plan so devious that I am sure you will approve. When I go into battle, tomorrow, I will not be dressed as Ahab, king of Israel. I will wear a disguise! The Syrians will try to kill some other poor fool and I shall escape, unharmed!'

Jezebel was appalled. And so upset that she could not eat a single mouthful more. After all her work, all her training, all her coaxing and encouraging and example-setting, had it come down to this? Her husband was not evil. Her husband was not wicked. He was a nasty little man, at best. And a coward, as well!

'All right, my dear,' she said, very quietly. 'Whatever you think is best.' But inwardly she hoped that she would never have to look at that face again.

Her wish came true, of course. Ahab disguised himself, just as he said he would. But a stray arrow struck him, anyway. He bled to death in his chariot, and when his servants washed the chariot down, they did so on the same spot where Naboth had died. And so Elijah's prophecy came true.

Some years later, a civil war broke out in Israel. The king's heirs and the king's commanders fought for control of the country, and in the end it was a man named Jehu who was victorious. Early one morning, he rode to Jezebel's house.

She knew he was coming. It was inevitable. So she put on her best clothes and make-up. 'He's a ruthless man,' she thought. 'Perhaps I can win him over and make him more ruthless still.'

But Jehu was ruthless enough already. When he saw Jezebel at the window, he called out to her servants and demanded that any who were loyal to him should seize her and throw her to the ground.

There were plenty of volunteers, as it happened, and while Jehu went into the house and had something to eat, the dogs breakfasted on the body of the dead queen.

'Someone had better bury that woman,' Jehu said to one of his servants, when he had finished. But when the servant went out into the street, there was nothing left to do. Elijah's prophecy had come true again—all that was left of Jezebel was her skull and her feet and the palms of her hands!

The Wicked Granny's Tale

▶ ▶ ▶ ▶ ▶ ▶ ▶ ▶ ▶ ▶ ▶ ▶ ▶

THE STORY OF ATHALIAH

My grandmother was pretty typical, as far as grannies go. She filled me up with sweets and cake and sugared cereal. She bought me far too many Christmas presents. And when I slept overnight at her house, she let me stay up well past my bedtime to watch scary movies!

She was also, for a very short time, one of my Sunday school teachers. And all I can imagine is that her passion for those Saturday night 'Mummy and Monster' movies must have spilled over onto her Sunday mornings, because she loved telling the most bloodthirsty Bible stories! Yes, that's when I first heard about Eglon and his sword-sucking stomach. Samson *and his crushing strength. And Judas, with his bowels gushing all over the ground. (I didn't even know what a bowel was, at the time—I just loved the way my grandmother said it!)*

Then, of course, there were the inevitable stories about Ahab, the evil Israelite king, and his foreign wife, Jezebel, who taught God's people all about the strange idols of her homeland, and persecuted the prophet Elijah, and whose blood was lapped up by the dogs when she died. And finally, there was Athaliah, the daughter of this wicked couple, who murdered her own grandchildren to gain control of the throne.

A wicked granny? An evil grandma? It seemed a strange thing, especially coming from my own grandmother's lips. Did it have any effect on me? Well, let's just say that, from that time on, I looked a little more suspiciously at the Frosted Flakes she fed me. And when those scary movies were over, I insisted on sleeping with the lights on—and my back right against the wall!

Sweet and gentle. Wise and kind. Kitchens rich with the smell of fresh-baked treats. That's what grannies are like!

But Athaliah was not your typical granny.

She was cruel and ambitious, deceitful and sly. And she had never baked a biscuit in her life! Evil plots were her speciality, and she cooked one up the moment she heard that her son, the king, was dead.

She gathered her guards around her. She whispered the recipe in their ears. And even though they were used to violence and to war, they could not hide the horror in their eyes.

'Yes, I know they're my grandsons,' Athaliah sneered.

'But I want you to kill them, so that I am sure to inherit the throne!'

Athaliah was not your typical granny. And she hadn't been much of a mother either. So perhaps that is why her daughter, Jehosheba, was not surprised when she peeped into the hallway and saw soldiers marching, swords drawn, towards the nursery door.

Jehosheba had a choice. She could rush to the nursery and throw herself in front of her little nephews—and be killed along with them, more likely than not. Or she could creep back into the room from which she'd come, and try to save the king's youngest son, Joash—the baby she'd been playing with when she had heard the soldiers pass.

The screams from the nursery answered her question. She was already too late, and she cursed the palace guards for their speed and efficiency. Speed was what she needed, as well, for she could hear the guards' voices coming her way.

'Did we get them all?'

'We'd better get them all!'

'The queen will have our heads if we've missed one.'

And so they burst into each room, one by one, down the long palace hall, and Jehosheba just had time to wrap her hand round the baby's mouth and duck into a cupboard.

'Don't cry,' she prayed, as the soldiers grunted and shuffled around the room. 'Please don't cry.'

'No one here,' someone said, at last. But Jehosheba stayed in that cupboard, as still as a statue, long after they had left the room. Then she wrapped up the baby in an old blanket and bundled him off to her home near the Temple.

Athaliah stared sternly at her soldiers.

'So you killed them? Every last one?' she asked.

'Every last one,' they grunted back. Athaliah's stare turned into an evil grin.

'Then tell me about it,' she ordered, 'and don't leave out one tiny detail.'

When the guards had finished their story, Athaliah sent them out of the room. Then she tossed back her head and cackled.

'At last. At last! AT LAST! Queen of Judah. Mother of the nation. That has a nice ring to it. And my parents... my parents would be so proud!'

Jehosheba's husband, Jehoiada, however, had a very different reaction.

'Well, what did you expect?' he fumed, when Jehosheba told him about the murder of their nephews. 'With a father like Ahab and a mother like Jezebel...'

'But I'm HER daughter!' Jehosheba protested. 'You don't mean to say...'

'No. NO!' Jehoiada assured her, as he wrapped his arms around his wife. 'I didn't mean that at all. You are a wonderful mother—a good woman who trusts in the God of Israel. And because of your love and courage, little Joash here is still alive.'

'The true ruler of Judah,' Jehosheba added. 'If only the people knew. You're the high priest. Perhaps you could tell them...'

'Even if they knew, they would do nothing.' Jehoiada sighed. 'Athaliah is much too powerful, and they are still entranced by the false gods she worships. No, we must wait—until they have seen through her evil ways. Then, and only then, dare we show this little fellow to them. Meanwhile, we shall hide him here, in the high priest's quarters, in the Temple of the our God. For this is the last place your wicked mother will want to visit.'

One year passed. And while little Joash learned to crawl and then to walk, his evil grandmother was busy murdering anyone who dared to take a step against her.

Two years passed. And as Joash spoke his first words and toddled around the Temple, Athaliah sang the praises of the false god Baal and offered him the blood of human sacrifice.

Three years, four years, five years passed. And as Joash grew into a little boy, the people of Judah grew tired of Athaliah's evil ways.

Six years passed. And when Joash was finally old enough to understand who he was, Jehoiada decided that the time had come to tell the nation, as well.

'We must be very careful,' he explained to his wife. 'The palace guards are finally on our side, but your mother still has some support among the people. We mustn't show our hand too soon.'

'So how will you do it?' Jehosheba asked.

'On the sabbath, it is the usual custom for two thirds of the palace guard to stay at the Temple while the others return to the palace to protect the queen. Tomorrow, however, the bodyguards will leave as expected, but they will not go to the palace. Instead they will return to the Temple by another route and help to protect young Joash, should anything happen.'

'Ah!' Jehosheba smiled. 'So Joash will be surrounded by the entire palace guard—while my mother will be left with no soldiers to carry out her orders!'

'Exactly!' Jehoiada grinned back.

When the sabbath came, the people gathered in the Temple, as usual, to worship the God of Israel. But there was nothing usual about what happened at the end of the service. Jehoiada, the high priest, led a little boy out in front of the crowd. Then he placed a crown on that little boy's head. And while the palace guard gathered round the child, the high priest shouted, 'Behold, people of Judah! Behold your true king—Joash, son of Ahaziah!'

All was silent for a moment, and then someone cheered. Someone else joined in and soon the cheering filled the Temple and echoed from there to the palace, where Athaliah was waiting, and wondering what had happened to her guards.

She was old and frail, now, but as wicked and as stubborn as ever!

'What's going on? What's all the noise about?' she muttered, as she hobbled out of the palace and across to the Temple.

'Out of my way! Get out of my way!' she ordered. And the crowd parted before her. And that's when something caught her eye—a glint, a gleaming from the little king's crown.

'What's the meaning of this?' she glared. 'This looks like treason to me!'

'Not treason, Athaliah,' said the high priest, 'but the true king of Judah restored to his rightful throne—Joash, your grandson!'

'My grandson?' Athaliah shuddered. 'But I thought... I mean... my soldiers... they told me...'

'That they had murdered them all?' asked Jehoiada. 'Is that what you meant to say? Well, in their haste to fulfil your wicked ambition, they missed one—the one who stands before you now, the true king of Judah!'

'Treason!' shouted the old woman again, but her words were stifled by the palace guards who quickly surrounded her.

'Where are we going? What are you doing?' she demanded to know, as they led her away. 'I'm an old woman—a grandmother—don't push me!'

'Don't worry, granny,' one of the guards whispered in her ear. 'This won't take long. Remember what you had us do to your grandsons all those years ago? Well we're going to do the same thing to you now!'

Athaliah shrieked, but only the guards heard her final cry, for the crowds were still cheering—cheering for Athaliah's grandson and for the end of her wicked reign.

The Proud Man's Tale

▷ ▷ ▷ ▷ ▷ ▷ ▷ ▷ ▷ ▷ ▷ ▷

THE STORY OF HAMAN

*P*ride's a funny thing. At first, it doesn't seem all that bad. Self-esteem with 'attitude'—that's what it looks like. But there's a difference.

Self-esteem is all about appreciating yourself for who you really are. It's based on honesty and truth. Pride, however, is rooted in self-deception, in a lie. It's all about convincing yourself that you're smarter or stronger or more important than you really are.

Take Haman, for example. He thought he was so important that he could destroy an entire race of people just because one member of that race had offended him. And, to be fair, he almost got away with it.

Ironically, though, it was that very same pride which tripped Haman up in the end. His confidence in his own *cleverness and power blinded him to the possibility that someone might actually be able to wreck his plans.*

And maybe that's the way it is with every kind of badness. At first, it looks as if the victims are the only ones who get hurt. But, in the end, the people who carry out the evil deeds are sometimes affected just as badly.

Haman walked through the King's Gate, nodding and waving as he went. The faces were familiar—royal officials, noblemen, important people, all of them, with whom he had worked and plotted and argued and fought. There were friends and there were enemies. There were wise men and there were fools. There were those who looked upon him with admiration and those who could barely hide their disgust. But each of them bowed as he passed, for Haman was now the second most powerful person in all of Persia— King Xerxes' right-hand man.

Haman grinned. And Haman strutted. A peacock would have struggled to match his pride. And then Haman came to the man at the end of the line.

'Ah yes, Mordecai,' he reminded himself. 'Mordecai the Jew. The one who uncovered a plot to kill the king—or something like that.' And he glanced at the man and tilted his head, ever so slightly, as if to say, 'Now. Now is the time for you to bow.'

But no bow came. Nor even the slightest hint of honour.

'I'm sorry,' said Mordecai. 'I bow to no man, but to the Lord God alone.'

Haman did nothing. He did not frown. He did not scowl. He did not stop and shout and swear. No, his face showed no emotion whatsoever. He simply walked on, careful to maintain his dignity. But inside, Haman was furious!

'How dare he?' Haman fumed. 'I will not stand for this insult! Mordecai, and all his people, will pay for the way he treated me today!'

And that is why, in the very first month of the next year, Haman went to see the king.

'Your Majesty,' he said, 'there is a certain group of people in our land—people who are different from the rest of us. They worship a different god. They keep different customs. And sometimes those customs require them to break our laws. They are the Jews, Your Majesty, and it seems to me that it would be in your best interest to have them—shall we say—'removed' from your kingdom. I feel so strongly about this, in fact, that I would be willing to put up ten thousand talents of my own silver to pay for their destruction.'

King Xerxes considered Haman's request. Then he took off his signet ring and gave it to his right-hand man.

'Do as you wish,' he said. 'And you can keep your money. If these people are as dangerous as you say, then it is the king's business to deal with them. Set the date. Seal the orders with my ring. And let the Jews be destroyed.'

Haman did as the king commanded. He wrote out orders for the destruction of the Jews and, being a superstitious man, he cast lots to determine on which day it should happen. When the lot fell on the twelfth month—the month of Adar—Haman was just a little disappointed. He would have to wait nearly a year for his revenge. And then he smiled, for the long wait meant that he would have the chance to gloat every time he walked past the King's Gate— every time he saw his insolent enemy, Mordecai.

What Haman did not know was that the God of Mordecai and his people had plans, as well. For, in spite of all his pride and self-importance, there was a tiny piece of information that the king's right-hand man did not possess.

And how could he, for it was unknown to the king, as well. But Mordecai knew it. And so did Mordecai's God. For it had to do with Mordecai's cousin, Hadassah, the most beautiful girl in the land!

Hadassah's mother and father were dead. So Mordecai had raised her, treating her like one of his own daughters. When King Xerxes had decided he needed a new wife, beautiful girls from all over the country came to Xerxes' harem. Among them was Hadassah, sent by Mordecai. He had given her a Persian name—Esther. And he had told her that she must, by no means, reveal that she was a Jew. (This was Mordecai's big secret.) And when the time had come for the king to choose his bride, Esther's beauty so overwhelmed him that the crown was placed on her head—and a Jewish girl became queen of all Persia!

When Mordecai heard about Haman's plot, he went immediately to Esther's palace. He stood outside the gates. He tore his clothes. He wept and he wailed. At once, Queen Esther sent her servant Hathach to find out what was the matter. Mordecai sent her this message: 'Haman plans to kill all the Jews in Persia. You must go the king and stop him!'

Esther sent a message back. It was not encouraging. 'You don't understand,' it read. 'I cannot go to the king unless he summons me. To go uninvited would be certain death! And I have not heard from him for a month.'

Mordecai's response was brief and plain: 'Don't think for a minute that you will escape just because you are the queen. If you do nothing, you will perish with the rest of us. But is it not possible that the Lord God has put you in your position for just such a time as this?'

So Esther agreed to go to see the king. She went uninvited and unannounced. And even though he could have put her to death for doing so, he was so taken with her beauty that he extended his golden sceptre in her direction and invited her to enter his throne room.

'What do you want, my dear?' King Xerxes asked.

'Only that you and your right-hand man, Haman, should join me for dinner,' she replied.

And so it was arranged. When he received the invitation, Haman was more puffed-up than ever.

'Look!' he said to his wife, Zeresh. 'Look!' he said to all his friends. 'An invitation to Queen Esther's table. Why, it's almost like I'm one of the family!'

So Haman went to dinner, and, as they were sipping their wine, King Xerxes turned to his queen and said, 'So tell me, my dear, why have you invited us here? I'll wager that there's something you want. You only have to ask, you know, and half my kingdom would be yours!'

Esther blushed and then she answered, mysteriously, 'My request is simple. Come again, tomorrow—you and your right-hand man, Haman—and I will tell you what I want.'

The king was intrigued. He liked this little game. And so, once again, he agreed.

Haman, meanwhile, couldn't believe his luck! Dinner at the queen's table two days in a row! But when he left the palace and passed the King's Gate, his mood turned suddenly sour. For there was Mordecai, again—Mordecai who refused to bow before him.

'You just wait!' Haman muttered to himself. 'The time will come when you will fall before me, begging for your life!'

He was still muttering when he arrived home. So his wife suggested a simple solution.

'Why wait till the end of the year to have Mordecai executed?' she asked. 'If he troubles you so, why not go to the king, first thing in the morning, and ask him to hang

Mordecai? Then you can enjoy your dinner with the queen and not worry about having to look on that insolent man's face again.'

Haman smiled—just a little at first. Then a huge grin broke out all over his face.

'Yes! Excellent!' he cried. And just so that everything would be ready, he ordered his servants to build a gallows, seventy-five feet high, in his own back garden!

The next morning, Haman strutted off to the king's palace, whistling as he went. There was no reason for Xerxes to deny his request. He was the king's right-hand man. So the order would be given, Mordecai would be executed, and this would be the happiest day of Haman's life!

But, once again, there was something that Haman did not know. Something he could never have guessed. Something that the God of Mordecai and his people would use to ensure that Haman's day did not turn out so well, after all.

King Xerxes had suffered through a sleepless night. And every time King Xerxes could not sleep, he ordered one of his servants to read to him from the *History of Persia*. And it just so happened that the passage the king's servant read on that night—the night before Haman's morning visit—was the passage that described how Mordecai had uncovered a plot to kill the king!

'Tell me,' King Xerxes said to his servant. 'Was Mordecai ever rewarded for this noble deed?'

'Not that I can remember,' answered the servant.

So the next morning, when Haman presented himself before the king, Xerxes asked him a question.

'What would you do if you wanted to honour a nobleman who had served you well?'

Puffed up as he was, Haman naturally assumed that the

king was referring to him. So he smiled broadly and offered the following suggestion: 'Take a royal robe that you yourself have worn and a royal horse that you yourself have ridden. Put the robe on the man, put the man on the horse, and then have some other royal official parade him through the city, shouting, "This is what happens to a man who earns the king's pleasure!" '

'An excellent idea!' the king shouted. 'Now I want you to do all that for Mordecai!'

'Mordecai?' Haman choked.

'Yes, Mordecai!' the king repeated. 'Put my robe on his back. Put him on my horse. And walk before him, announcing to everyone what happens to the man who earns my pleasure!'

Haman nodded. Haman bowed. Haman tried very hard not to cringe. Then Haman did what the king commanded, growing angrier with every royal hoofbeat!

When he returned home and told his wife what had happened, she sighed and shook her head.

'It would be foolish to ask for his execution, now. The God Mordecai serves must be very powerful, indeed. The best you can do is enjoy your dinner with the queen and pray that nothing worse happens.'

So Haman went to Queen Esther's palace. But he did not strut. And he did not whistle. He walked with his head lowered, hoping to avoid the wrath of Mordecai's God.

All seemed well at dinner, however. There was laughing and there was joking and Haman's mood began to brighten. Then, over a goblet of wine, King Xerxes turned to his wife and asked, 'So why have you invited us again, my dear? Tell me what you wish for. You may ask for anything—up to half of my kingdom—and it will be yours.'

Queen Esther's suddenly looked serious. Tears filled her eyes.

'Your Majesty,' she said, 'there is someone who wants to destroy me—me and all my people. He has already signed the orders, the date has already been set, and unless you do something to spare us, in the twelfth month, the month of Adar, we will all die!'

The king's face turned serious, too—then red with rage.

'Who has done this thing?' he shouted. 'Tell me and he is the one who will die!'

Esther turned her head slowly and looked straight at a trembling Haman.

'I know this may come as a surprise,' she said, 'but I am a Jew, Your Majesty. And the person who wants to kill me— me and all my people—is your own right-hand man.' And then she pointed. 'It is Haman.'

King Xerxes banged his fist on the table, spilling his wine. He loved his wife—his beautiful wife. And yet, he had signed the order. So he stormed out into the garden to think.

Haman was no fool. He could see what was coming. So when Queen Esther rose from the table and walked away to wait on her couch, he followed her, then threw himself on the couch beside her, begging for mercy. It was at that moment that the king returned to the room.

'What is this?' he cried. 'First you want to kill my wife, and now you make advances to her?'

'No, Your Majesty...' Haman stuttered. But before he could finish his sentence, King Xerxes had called for his guards.

'Reverse the order to destroy the Jews,' he announced. 'And put this man to death, instead!'

'As you wish, Your Majesty,' said the chief guard. And then he added, 'There is already a gallows prepared. At Haman's house, in fact. Rumour has it that he built it for

Mordecai, who saved the king's life.'

'Then hang Haman on it!' the king commanded. 'And let this be a lesson for anyone who displeases the king!'

So Haman was hanged, the Jews were saved, and Queen Esther became a hero to her people—a hero whose deeds are celebrated to this day!

The Traitor's Tale

• • • • • • • • • • • •

THE STORY OF JUDAS

So why did he do it? Why did Judas betray Jesus? People have been asking that question ever since those thirty pieces of silver changed hands. And they have come up with a lot of different answers.

Some have suggested that even though Judas was a follower of Jesus—one of his twelve disciples—he simply misunderstood what Jesus was all about. Others have pointed to the money. Or to the influence of the devil. And some have argued that the reason was political—that Judas was originally part of a revolutionary movement that wanted to overthrow the Romans and believed that Jesus would help that cause. And that the betrayal was a result of Judas' frustration when he realized that was not Jesus' intent at all. Finally, there are those who suggest that it was all somehow God's fault—

that someone had to do the deed and it was Judas' fate to be the one.

As you will see in the following story, I think there is a case to be made for some of these arguments. Except for the last one, that is.

Judas made a decision. He may have been tempted to do it. But he was not forced. Not by God. Not by fate. Not by anyone. His motives may have been pure, they may have been selfish, they may have been confused. But the inescapable fact is this: regardless of Judas' reason for betraying Jesus, that betrayal resulted in Jesus' death.

'He's just not practical!' moaned Judas. 'I think my objection basically boils down to that.'

Judas' companion nodded his head, sympathetically. 'I can see your problem,' he said. 'The man is unfamiliar with the ways of the world.'

'Exactly!' Judas agreed, banging his hand on the table. 'I knew you would understand.' The disciple liked this man. He was a minor official on the Temple staff—the assistant to the assistant to the assistant of the high priest, or something like that. Judas had met him quite by chance, but they had 'clicked' almost at once. The man was confident, persuasive, poised. And best of all, he seemed to sympathize with the disciple's ever-growing frustration.

'Lofty sentiments. High ideals,' the companion went on. 'But it takes more than that to change the world, doesn't it?'

'It's what I've been saying for years,' the disciple sighed. 'But no one wants to listen. Least of all him! We need a power-base, I argue. We need to solidify our following. We need a realistic plan...'

'You need money,' added the companion.

'Money!' the disciple sighed again. 'Don't talk to me about money. Talk to him! He treats it like it was leprosy! No, I take that back—he treats lepers better than he treats your average rich man.'

The companion leaned forward, intrigued. 'How so?'

Judas sighed. 'Where do I start? There are so many examples. All right, here's one:

'This fellow comes along, one day. He's rich—it's obvious. His clothes. His jewellery. The way he walks and holds his head. He wants to join us, so he asks Jesus what he has to do. No, no, first he calls Jesus "Good Teacher". That's it. And Jesus has to go on and on about nobody being good but God. I mean, give me a break. Jesus is about as good as they come. But can he take a compliment? Can he just get on with the conversation? No.'

'The point, my friend?' the companion interrupted. 'What is the point?'

'Yes, well, after all the "song and dance" about goodness, this fellow asks Jesus what he needs to do to get into the kingdom of heaven. Jesus tells him all the obvious stuff: obey the commandments, love your neighbour, blah, blah, blah. The man says he's done all that (the rest of us look at each other and roll our eyes—"Yeah, right!"). But instead of challenging him on that, Jesus tells him that there is just one more thing he needs to do. He has to sell everything he has, and give it the poor.'

'And...?' the companion asked, leaning even further forward.

'What do you think?' the disciple shrugged. 'He walked away.'

'And did Jesus go after him?'

'Of course not!' sighed Judas. 'He just turned to the rest

of us and went on about how hard it is for rich men to get into the kingdom of heaven. "Harder than squeezing a camel through the eye of a needle." Those were his exact words.'

The companion stroked his chin. 'That concerns me,' he said seriously. 'It doesn't seem right, somehow.'

Now the disciple leaned forward. 'You know, there were a few of us who thought the same thing. I don't know about you, but I have always been taught that wealth is a sign of God's blessing. Not Jesus! He acts as if it's some kind of curse.'

'Unless one uses it to help the poor,' the companion added.

'Well, yes... and no,' Judas sighed. 'There was this other time. A woman came to Jesus and started to pour this bottle of incredibly expensive perfume on his feet.'

'Quite a luxury!' the companion observed.

'Exactly,' agreed Judas. 'And the first thing that came to my mind was our little treasury. We needed funds desperately, and I, of all people, knew that.'

'What with you being the treasurer?' the companion interrupted.

'Just so. Anyway, I knew that I would get nowhere if I suggested selling the perfume and putting the profits in our money bag. So I simply suggested that we sell it and give the money (well, some of the money!) to the poor. Foolproof, I thought—a perfectly reasonable plan. But, no! Jesus has a different idea. "The poor will always be with us," he says. "But I am only going to be here for a short while." Who knows what he meant by that? "So leave the woman alone and let her get on with it."

'Now you tell me. Is there any consistency in that, whatsoever? Anything sensible? Anything practical? On the one hand, he accepts this expensive gift. On the other, he condemns rich men for their wealth.'

The companion shook his head. 'It makes no sense to me—particularly since there are rich men who belong to your little band of followers. What about Levi, the one they call Matthew?'

Judas rolled his eyes. 'The tax collector. Yes, well, we seem to specialize in those. Matthew. Zacchaeus. But it's always the same drill: make friends with Jesus. Give all your money away. Pay back the ones you've cheated. Help the poor. And by the time it's over, there's nothing left for our little treasury. And I should know…'

'What with you being the treasurer,' the companion said again.

'Exactly!' sighed the disciple. 'And if Jesus ever took the time to look into our money bag, he'd understand what I have to deal with. It takes more than a penny or two to change the world. And besides, I don't trust him.'

'Jesus?' asked the companion.

'No! No! Matthew!' replied Judas. 'I think he's still in league with the Romans. It makes sense, doesn't it? He collected taxes for the Romans for all those years. And now I catch him taking notes on what we're up to. Watching, listening, and then scribbling things down! He's spying for them, I'm sure of it.'

'I can see why you might be concerned,' the companion said. 'The Romans are a worry.'

'The main worry!' Judas cried. 'It's why I joined up with Jesus in the first place. If he is the Messiah—and the miracles alone are enough to convince me of that—then he will eventually destroy the Romans and our land will be free again. I just wish he'd get on with it. Forget all this nonsense about love and forgiveness for a while, and start dealing with more practical matters—like raising an army and putting together some kind of battle plan...'

'And finding the money,' the companion added.

'And finding the money,' Judas sighed.

'This is dangerous talk,' the companion whispered. Then he leaned forward and whispered more quietly still, so that his whisper sounded almost like a hiss. 'But I think I may have a way to help you.'

'Really?' the disciple whispered back.

'Yes,' the companion continued. 'Some of my employers in the high priest's office would like to have a word with Jesus. Privately. They, too, are concerned about the direction his teaching has taken and feel that if they could just spend some time alone with him, that they might be able to get him back on the right track. If you could lead them to some quiet spot where they could meet with him, I am sure that they would reward you handsomely.'

'How handsomely?' Judas asked.

The companion smiled. 'I keep forgetting that I am dealing with a practical man here, my friend.' And then he paused and then he thought. He had the look of man bartering for some great treasure. 'What would you say to... oh... thirty pieces of silver?'

Judas' eyes lit up. 'I would say, "You have a deal!" '

The companion stood and reached out his hand.

'So I can count on you?' he asked.

'Of course,' Judas answered. 'At the first opportunity. And the money...?'

'Trust me,' the companion smiled. 'It'll be fine.'

And as he walked away, Judas smiled, as well. Everything was back on course. Plans, programmes, practical matters. And finally the money to make it happen.

'Thirty pieces of silver,' he grinned. 'With that kind of money, I can really make a difference in the world!'

The Magician's Tale

Simon was jealous. It was as simple as that. Somebody had something he wanted. Not a possession. Not a position. Not even a person. No, it was power—power to make the lame walk and the blind see.

His jealousy ate at him. And that ugly mix of frustration, disappointment, anger and bitterness blinded him to everything but his own desire. And led him to do something terrible. That's the way it is with jealousy. Sometimes the jealousy itself makes it even harder to get what we want.

The sad thing is that, in time, the very thing that Simon wanted might well have been his for the asking.

But it was not for the grabbing.

It was not for the taking.

And it was certainly not his for the buying.

Whenever Simon walked through the streets of Samaria, people stopped and took notice.

Sometimes they pointed.

Sometimes they bowed.

Sometimes they found the courage to wave hello.

And sometimes they even shouted, 'Look, there goes the Great Power of God!'

Simon loved every minute of it! He didn't show it, of course. It would have spoiled the air of mystery and awe he had worked so hard to create. So he would nod, and stretch forth his hand—ever so slightly—like a king waving to his subjects.

But Simon was no king, nor royalty of any kind, for that matter. No, Simon was a sorcerer. Or, to be more precise, he had quick hands, a way with healing potions, and a knack for making predictions that, more often than not, came true. Magician? Rogue? Call it what you like—Simon's chosen 'occupation' had brought him fame and wealth and power, and, as far as he was concerned, that was all that mattered.

And then, suddenly, one day, everything changed.

Simon walked through the streets of Samaria, and nobody noticed.

Nobody pointed.

Nobody bowed.

Nobody said, 'There goes the Great Power of God!'

For the streets were empty and there was nobody there. Well, almost nobody. A boy ran past Simon, nearly knocking him down along the way.

'What's the hurry?' Simon called.

'It's the miracle man!' the boy shouted back over his shoulder. 'He's in the fields on the edge of town!'

'A miracle man?' Simon grumbled to himself. 'The last thing I need is competition. But what should I do?' he wondered. 'Should I ignore the man completely? Or should I hang about at the edge of the crowd, have a good look at his bag of tricks, and then make him look a fool in front of everyone?'

As Simon pondered this question, someone else rushed by, bumping into him. It was Nathan, the town baker.

'Beg your pardon,' he muttered. 'But... well... at the edge of town...'

'Yes, I know,' said Simon, with a condescending smile. 'A miracle man—or so they say.'

'Oh, he's a miracle man, all right!' the baker answered. 'Blind folk see! Lame folk walk! Come and see for yourself.'

'Yes, I think I'll do just that,' said Simon, the smile dropping from his face.

The baker rushed off again. But Simon took his time. There was a part of him that wanted very much to see this miracle man, and another part that was afraid of seeing him at all.

When Simon finally reached the crowd, no one even noticed him. No one pointed or bowed or waved. For every eye was trained on the man at the front.

'He doesn't look like much of a sorcerer,' Simon thought. 'Those robes are far too plain and his gestures much too awkward.'

Old Hannah, who had walked with a limp for years, stepped forward and held her hands out to the miracle man. And Simon just rolled his eyes.

'Good luck with that one!' he thought. 'A dozen healing potions—and all she can do is complain about the taste!'

The man took hold of Hannah's hands. He bowed his head and shut his eyes and whispered some kind of spell— or at least that's what it looked like to Simon.

'Where's the drama?' Simon wondered. 'Where's the

72

flair?' And then he grunted, so that everyone around him could hear, 'Not exactly a real magician, if you ask me.' And he turned to walk away.

But at that moment, a cheer burst forth from the crowd!

Simon turned back to look—and there was Hannah, leaping and dancing as if she was nine years old!

'It's amazing!' someone shouted.

'It's a miracle!' shouted someone else.

And then someone at the front shouted something that made Simon cringe.

'This man must be the Great Power of God!'

Now Simon wanted to shout as well. He wanted to shout, 'No! This man is not the Great Power of God! I am!'

But much to his surprise the miracle man said it for him.

'Please don't call me that,' he said. 'I am not the Great Power of God, or any power at all. My name is Philip. I am a follower of Jesus of Nazareth, and it is through his power that this woman has been healed.'

Simon was shocked. If he had made old Hannah walk, he would have raised his arms to the sky and commanded the crowd to fall at his feet. And they would have—he was sure of it! But this man? What was this man up to? What did he want?

'I only want to talk to you,' Philip continued, 'to tell you about this Jesus whom I follow.' And to Simon's amazement, that's exactly what he did. He took no money. He asked no favours. He simply went on healing people, and as he did so, he told them about a man named Jesus.

'Jesus was God's own Son,' Philip explained. Then he laid his hands on a troubled man, who screamed and then smiled gently as if something bad had left him. 'Jesus came to overcome evil. He came so that people could be part of his kingdom—a kingdom of goodness and peace.

'Jesus was a teacher, too.' Philip went on. And as a little girl who had been blind looked for the first time at her mother, Philip said, 'We are all blind, in our own way. Jesus came to help us see more clearly what's important and to show us the truth about God and life and love.'

Simon listened carefully as Philip lowered his voice.

'Sadly,' Philip sighed, 'there were people who did not like Jesus. So they crucified him and buried him in a tomb.'

The crowd sighed along with him and then watched as a smile broke out on his face.

'But God would not let that be the end of the story,' he said with a grin. 'So, three days later, he raised Jesus from the dead! I know people who saw him. And now that he has gone back to be with his Father in heaven, he wants all of us to follow him and be part of his kingdom of love!'

Simon watched as the people streamed towards Philip. He was having trouble making sense of any of this. But there was one thing he knew for certain—there was no way that his own power could even begin to compare with the power of this Philip, or the Jesus he spoke of. And if he couldn't beat them, then there was only one choice left. He would have to join them, and get hold of this power for himself.

Several days went by, and Simon stayed as close to Philip as he possibly could. He listened closely to Philip's prayers (they were definitely not spells, Philip had explained politely). He carefully watched Philip's movements. But, try as he might, Simon could not make the power of Jesus work for him.

Simon was disappointed. Simon was frustrated. And it didn't help that everyone's attention was still focused on Philip. That is, until two of Philip's friends came to town.

'The older one is Peter,' Philip explained to Simon. 'And the younger one is John. Both of these men were Jesus' disciples. They lived and worked with him for three years. They saw him when he rose from the dead. And now they have come here from Jerusalem to pray for all the new believers.'

Simon watched these two men, and as far as he could tell, they didn't look any more special than Philip. 'Why,' Simon thought, 'the older one looks just like a common labourer or fisherman!'

Philip, however, treated them with the utmost respect. And as soon as they began praying and placing their hands on the believers, Simon understood why. For the most amazing things began to happen.

Some people fainted dead away. Some began speaking in other languages. And others just leaped up and down for joy.

Simon listened carefully, and he heard the two men say the exact same words, 'May the Lord fill you with his Holy Spirit.'

'Aha!' Simon thought. 'That's the secret. The power lies in this Holy Spirit.' And as soon as he got the chance, he took Peter and John aside. He'd had a good look at them. Maybe Philip hadn't wanted any money, but these men (the older one in particular) looked as if they could use a set of new clothes. And so he bowed and said, as humbly as he could, 'I, too, would like to have the power to pass on this Holy Spirit. How much would it cost to buy it from you?'

Peter looked at John. John looked at Peter. And Simon thought, for a moment that they might ask for time to talk together about the price. But when Peter gave his answer, Simon realized that he had got it all wrong, again!

'A curse on you and your money!' Peter shouted. And Simon shrank back at the force of his words. 'The Holy Spirit is God's free gift!' Peter went on. 'And to offer to buy it with money shows that your heart is not right with God at all. I can see you are full of bitterness and jealousy. And the best thing you can do is ask God's forgiveness for what you have done!'

If Simon had thought about it, for even a minute, he would have seen that Peter was right. Bitterness—at losing his fame and power and attention—had been driving him all along. But Simon had only heard the curse. And he thought that someone powerful enough to bless the blind and the lame could make his curses come true as well. So he begged Peter to remove the curse and then hurried away from the crowd.

No one knows for certain what happened to Simon. But there is an old story which suggests that his bitterness never did go away. The story says that Simon took his bag of tricks to other places in the ancient world, and that he managed to rebuild his reputation. But then one day, many years later, he ran into Peter again. Still angry over his embarrassment in Samaria, he challenged Peter to a contest.

'You say that this Jesus was buried in the earth for three days and then rose again. To prove that I am even greater than he, I will be buried, as well. And I, too, shall rise in three days.'

That's what Simon did, so the story goes. He had himself buried in the ground. And as far as anyone knows, he's buried there still!

The Fanatic's Tale

● ● ● ● ● ● ● ● ● ● ● ● ●

THE STORY OF PAUL

Sometimes people do the wrong things for the wrong reason. They steal because they are greedy. They lie because they don't want to get caught. They cheat because they are too lazy to do their own work.

But there is another reason that people sometimes do what is wrong. The right reason. So they think anyway.

Saul was one of those people. He wanted to please God, and serve God, and live his life for God. But he found himself threatening and torturing and even killing, all in the name of God. All for the 'right' reason. The problem was that Saul misunderstood God, as so many do when they use force or violence to try to do God's will. When Saul finally 'met' God, he realized how wrong he had been. He saw a God working not through brutal force but through kindness and love, mercy and forgiveness.

He took the garments, one by one, and hung them over his arm. Shoulder to shoulder, he folded them. Crease to crease. Sleeve to sleeve. Each one neat. Each one straight. Each one perfect.

Saul knew that his was a small contribution. But on the road to perfection, every detail mattered. And even the tiniest step in the wrong direction could send one wandering off the path for ever.

No further proof was needed than the man on the ground before him. Saul had listened carefully to Stephen's speech. The man knew the scriptures well. From Abraham to Moses, from Joshua to David, he had rehearsed the history of Israel with passion and poise. Every point was well argued, every detail well described. But then there was the mis-step. He raised his voice. He pointed his finger. And finally Stephen accused the council of murdering the long-awaited Messiah!

How could Stephen have been so foolish? How could he have wandered so far from the truth? 'Stiff-necked', that's what he had called the council—'murderers'! And over what? The death of a blasphemous carpenter from Galilee, who had gone against everything that Saul believed by teaching that he was more important than Moses or the Temple or God's own Law.

Jesus had deserved to die. The Law of God demanded it. And this man—this Stephen—deserved no less.

The rocks were crashing down upon him, even now—cracking his head and his limbs, crushing the life out of him. And his sweaty executioners would soon want their robes back. So Saul stood and held their garments and watched Stephen calling out his blasphemy, 'Receive my spirit, Lord Jesus!' (as if this Jesus were God himself!) until he breathed his last.

'Jesus!' Saul soon came to hate that name. Stephen's death did nothing to slow the spread of that blasphemer's teachings, and Saul was convinced that something needed to be done. He knew that false teaching could be as strong as the truth. And this particular teaching was like a cancer—popping up here and there, all over Judea—infecting one community after another.

It had to be stopped. And Saul knew that he was the man to do it.

He had the background—a long and noble family tradition.

He had the education—there was no finer teacher than his master, the Pharisee Gamaliel.

And most of all, he had the discipline. 'A Pharisee's Pharisee'—that's what someone had called him once. And he had taken it as a compliment. Yes, he'd heard the whispers about some of the teachers—'those Pharisees are proud, they're holier-than-thou.' But he had always assumed that was nothing more than jealousy. Right beliefs. Right actions. That's what God demanded. And surely every community needed individuals who were willing to sacrifice everything so that everyone could see what believing the right thing and doing the right thing would look like if it were lived out day by day.

Saul was such an individual. And he was convinced that only a person like him—dedicated to observing the tiniest details of the Law—could stand against the spread of this false teaching. This was the job he'd been born for. Now he could show, once and for all, his absolute devotion to God.

And so Saul set to work. Some of Jesus' followers he arrested and sent to jail. Others he threatened with violence. Still others he beat. And some he even put to death!

It was hard work. It was tiring. And it was far from pleasant. Torture and threats and death brought Saul no joy. In fact, there were times when the whole thing nearly broke his heart. The followers of Jesus were devoted people— passionate about their faith. In different circumstances, he might have called them his brothers and sisters.

But they were wrong! What they believed was wrong! They had taken a mere man and set him up beside God himself! And God would not stand for that. Such arrogance, such sin, would have to be punished. That is what the Law said. That is how God worked. And there was no way around it.

And so Saul went on—the instrument of God's punishment. And his efficiency and attention to detail soon made him the man most feared by the followers of Jesus. In spite of his hard work, however, the heresy continued to spread. And when word reached him that it had even travelled up north to Damascus, he went straight to the high priest and asked for permission to seek out the blasphemers and bring them to Jerusalem to face trial.

It was a long trip to Damascus—a hundred miles or so. And Saul was looking forward to the journey's end. Partly because he was tired. And partly because he could not wait to get to work. But as the noonday sun shone down upon his head, he noticed that it was brighter than he had ever seen it before. And then suddenly the light burned brighter still and shone so piercing and white that Saul shut his eyes and fell frightened to the ground.

Words came next—ringing in his ears and banging in his skull.

'Saul! Saul!' the voice pleaded. 'Why do you persecute me, Saul?'

Saul blinked, struggling to understand. 'Persecute?' he thought. 'Surely this voice, this voice from heaven, can't mean me. I teach people and guide them. I am a defender of the One True God!'

And so Saul asked, 'Who are you, Lord?' And the voice answered plainly with the last name Saul expected to hear.

'Jesus,' the voice said. 'I am Jesus. And you are my persecutor.'

On his knees, on the ground, all Saul could think of was Stephen—that other man on his knees, that other man on the ground, with the robes of his executioners in Saul's hands. What had Stephen said before he died? Whom had he called out to? The same voice, the same name, the same light that now blinded Saul. And it was at that moment that Saul's life—like a garment that was ironed and straight and perfect, down to the smallest detail—began to unravel and unfold.

Stephen was not the blasphemer. Stephen was not the one who had got it all wrong. It was Saul, himself, who had wandered off God's path—Saul, God's defender, who had been persecuting God's Messiah all along!

How could he have been so foolish? How could he have been so wrong? Saul folded himself into a bundle—a crumpled pile of sadness and shame. And as the voice commanded him to go to Damascus and wait, his companions pulled him, shaking, to his feet, and discovered that he could no longer see.

It didn't matter to Saul, not really. In spite of his efforts, his very best efforts—his hard work and his sacrifices and his attention to detail—he had still, somehow, managed to do the very opposite of what God wanted. Blindness was the least he deserved.

Blindness, in fact, was almost a kind of refuge. For it kept him from having to face those companions who had looked to him as their model.

For one day, he fasted. No food and no drink. And the enormity of his failure overwhelmed him.

For a second day, he fasted. And the failure was followed by fear and despair.

For a third day, he fasted, and prayed the whole day for God's mercy, convinced, all the while, that his sin would result in one thing only—God's anger. And God's punishment.

And then there came another vision. It started with a visitor and a knock at the door. The visitor's name was Ananias. He was a follower of Jesus. And when he spoke, his voice shook, but Saul could not tell whether it was from anger or from fear.

Saul expected the worst. It was what he deserved. And when his companions protested that he should have nothing to do with this man, Saul shooed them away and quietly asked Ananias to stay.

The vision went on, as Ananias walked slowly towards Saul. And when Ananias' hands landed on Saul's shoulders, both men trembled.

'This is it,' thought Saul. 'I have murdered this man's brothers and sisters. I have beaten them and dragged them off to prison. Wrongly, wrongly have I acted, and now I must face God's punishment.'

'Brother Saul,' Ananias began. And Saul could hardly believe his ears.

'Brother? Brother?!'

'It was the Lord Jesus you saw on the road,' Ananias continued, 'and it was the same Lord Jesus who sent me here to speak with you. He wants you to see again.' The vision ended, and it wasn't long before a real knock came at the front door. It was the same man—Ananias—and, step by step, the dream played itself out before him, until Ananias laid his hands on Saul's shoulders—and he could see!

Saul looked for the first time into Ananias' eyes, and he watched his mouth speak the words he'd only dreamed of hearing.

'It was God himself who did this,' Ananias explained. 'The God of our fathers, Abraham, Isaac and Jacob. He has chosen you, Saul. Chosen you to see the risen Lord, chosen you to hear his voice, and chosen you to tell the whole world of his love and his mercy. So taste his mercy yourself, Saul. Get up. Be baptized. Call upon his name and let him wash away your sins.'

The water felt good. Up over his knees and his waist it flowed. Up further past his chest and face. He was buried beneath the water. And when he rose up again and gasped for his first breath, he knew that he had left something behind in that water for ever. The old Saul was down there, the Saul who'd believed that he could somehow earn God's approval by his efforts, his good works, his attention to detail. The Saul who had almost let his proud devotion to God blind him to the most important thing of all—God's mercy and forgiveness.

And so he came up out of that water a new man. With a new mission. And soon he would have a new name. He would be Paul now, not Saul. And his life would be devoted to helping others find God's mercy and forgiveness, as well.

The Liars' Tale

• • • • • • • • • • • • • •

THE STORY OF
ANANIAS AND SAPPHIRA

*S*ome say that lying is no big deal. 'Everybody does it!' they
suggest. And sadly, even government leaders sometimes try
to convince people that certain lies are all right so that they
keep their positions of power.

    *The interesting thing is that those kinds of excuses
usually come from the people who do the lying. People who get
lied to often have a different opinion. They feel disappointed,
angry, betrayed, and they sometimes have difficulty trusting
people again.*

    *Lying hurts. And if you have ever been lied to, you
know exactly what I mean. That's because lying is mostly
rooted in selfishness. We do it to protect ourselves or—as you
will see in the following story—to impress somebody else.*

Yes, everybody does it. But lying is still wrong. And it's definitely a big deal. As a man named Ananias (not the Ananias who befriended Paul!) and his wife, Sapphira, came to discover…

'So what did you think of the sermon, dear?' Ananias asked his wife, Sapphira as they walked along to their friends' house.

'Very… interesting,' she answered, choosing the word carefully. 'And you?'

'A little long-winded, I thought,' said Ananias. 'Nothing against Peter, of course. He's a capable speaker, on the whole, but… well…'

'I know just what you mean,' his wife responded. 'The lack of education shows. We've all noticed it. Why, some of the ladies and I were talking about it just the other day. But he has other qualities.'

'That's just what I was going to say,' agreed Ananias. 'Enthusiasm, passion…'

'And punctuality!' Sapphira added. 'I think that's very important in a church leader.'

Ananias chuckled. 'Yes, well, you should know, dear.'

'No one's perfect,' Sapphira frowned. 'And besides, I'm getting better. I'm not nearly as late for things as I used to be.'

Ananias glanced at the sun. 'Well, here's your chance to prove it,' he said. 'If we don't hurry, we're going to be late for dinner with the Bar-Josephs!'

Sapphira frowned again and slowed her pace. 'But they're so… intense!' she moaned. 'With their "Hallelujah!" this, and their "Praise the Lord!" that.'

'Levi and Hannah Bar-Joseph are important members of

the church,' Ananias explained. 'Second cousins to the apostle Bartholomew! So if we want to get ahead in the church then we have to get on with them.'

'But the "hallelujahs"!' Sapphira countered.

'Just hold your tongue and smile,' Ananias ordered. 'Now hurry!'

Dinner at the Bar-Josephs was exceptional. But, as they feared, Ananias and Sapphira found the conversation much more difficult to swallow.

'I was truly blessed by the sermon today!' said Hannah Bar-Joseph enthusiastically.

'Hallelujah!' added her husband, Levi.

'Why, I could listen to Peter all day long!' she went on.

'Praise the Lord!' Levi shouted.

'God is going to use that man in a powerful way!' she concluded.

And Levi managed to squeeze in one more 'hallelujah' before his 'Amen'.

Ananias glanced at Sapphira. He could see the corners of her mouth start to quiver. So he quickly changed the subject.

'There were a lot of new people at worship today,' he noted.

'More every week!' Hannah smiled.

But before her husband could add yet another 'hallelujah', Sapphira spoke up. 'Don't you think we have to be the tiniest bit careful, though?' she asked. 'All these new people, I mean. There were a few sitting behind me, today. Nothing but rags on. And their children—sniffling and coughing and making all kinds of noise. Why, I could hardly hear Peter's excellent sermon. They're just not the sort... well, you know what I'm saying.'

A silence descended on the room. Ananias noted the

shocked expressions on the faces of his hosts. If he had been sitting next to his wife, he would have nudged her, or poked her, or even given her a quick kick on the shins. But that was out of the question, so hastily he jumped back into the conversation.

'What my wife means to say is that there are so many of these poor souls for us to care for.' Then Ananias hesitated, weighing his words carefully. 'And care for them, we must... as Jesus would... care for them,' he added finally.

Hannah looked at Levi.

Levi looked at Hannah.

And then, together, both of them shouted, 'Hallelujah!'

And Ananias breathed a quiet sigh of relief.

'Oh, but you know there is a way we can care for these poor souls,' said Hannah. 'I'm sure you've heard. Everyone is selling their things. Jewellery, clothing, even houses and land. Why, just today, I heard that Barnabas, that sweet man, sold a very nice piece of property. And all that money will go into a common fund to meet the needs of just the kinds of folk that you described.'

Ananias looked at Sapphira.

Sapphira fingered the shiny bracelet round her wrist.

Neither of them had ever heard of such a thing. Both of them were horrified at the thought. But admitting that to the Bar-Josephs was simply not an option. So Ananias just smiled and said, 'What a splendid idea!'

'Yes, how inventive,' added Sapphira, slowly slipping the bracelet up under the end of her sleeve.

'To be honest,' said Levi, 'that is one of the reasons we invited you to dinner today. We understand that you own a field or two out in the country and wondered if you might part with one of them and give the money to help these poor people?'

Another silence descended on the group, and this time it was Ananias and Sapphira who looked nervously at each other.

Ananias cleared his throat. 'Well, that would certainly be something to think about,' he said slowly.

'Yes, to *think* about,' said Sapphira, more deliberately. 'On our way *home*,' she added, hoping that, in his present state of shock, Ananias would still be able to catch the hint.

'Home. Yes,' repeated Ananias. 'It's about time, isn't it? Lovely meal. Thanks very much. And we'll let you know— um...'

'At the next gathering?' suggested Hannah.

'All right then,' Ananias smiled weakly.

'Amen to that!' shouted Levi.

And Ananias and Sapphira staggered out of the door for home.

'Well, *I've* thought about it,' grunted Sapphira, when they were no more than a minute's walk down the road. 'And I think it's the stupidest thing I've ever heard!'

'What?' Ananias grunted back. 'More stupid than insulting the poor and needy in front of holy Hannah back there? If you hadn't opened your mouth, we wouldn't be in this mess at all!'

'Oh, really?' Sapphira snapped back. 'You heard them— that's why they invited us! "They're important!" you said. "We have to get on with them," you said. Well look where it's got us! More noisy children! More stinking beggars! More ruined worship! And we have to pay for it!!'

'That's enough!' snapped Ananias. 'There's a way out of this.' Then he stopped. Then he smiled. 'And I may have just thought of it!'

'Well, hallelujah!' Sapphira sneered.

But Ananias ignored her and went on. 'Nobody really

knows what our land is worth, do they?'

'Well, I should hope *you* know!' Sapphira grunted.

'Of course I know,' sighed Ananias. 'The point is that no one else knows! So why don't we simply sell the land for what it's worth, keep half for ourselves and give away the other half?'

Sapphira's eyes lit up. 'That's brilliant!' she said. 'We keep part of what really belongs to us, anyway, and we still manage to impress Hannah and Levi and all the rest!'

Ananias paused. 'My only real concern is Peter. We're going to have to lie to him, after all. I hope he doesn't catch on.'

Sapphira smiled and tapped the side of her head. 'He's not too bright, remember? We've got nothing to worry about there. And besides, it's not really lying. We'll say something like, "Here's what we got for the land." And then it's all down to what the meaning of the word "got" is, isn't it?'

Sapphira shook her bracelet out from under her sleeve. She took her husband's hand. And they walked home together happily.

The next Sunday, Sapphira was late, as usual. Late getting up. Late dressing. Late for breakfast. And so, Ananias left without her, as he always did.

'Just remember to keep the story straight!' he shouted, as he stormed out of the door. 'And thanks for going out of your way to be so supportive!'

Sapphira grinned. Being late today was more than just a bad habit. She was a lousy liar and she knew it. So why not let Ananias do the 'dirty work' and show up later for all the praise!

Ananias was sweating by the time he got to the meeting place.

'There's no reason to be nervous,' he assured himself.

And he smiled and waved at the Bar-Josephs and held up his money bag. 'The deal was done very quietly,' he thought. 'The buyer lives in another town. There's no way that anyone could know.'

So he sang the psalms and listened to the sermon and then rose to join the queue with the others who had sold their belongings.

Ananias waited impatiently, wiping the sweat from his forehead and wishing this was over. He watched the others, he worked up his nerve, and he consoled himself with thoughts of how impressed everyone would be. Finally, it was his turn.

This was the first time that Ananias had been so close to Peter. He was surprised by the man's height. And even more surprised by the look in his eye. Sapphira was wrong. This man was no fool. And Ananias was not comforted by that thought—not at all.

'I... that is, we... my wife and I,' Ananias stammered, 'we sold a piece of land. And here is the money we got for it.'

Peter looked at Ananias, deep into his eyes. A drop of sweat fell from Ananias' forehead and rolled down one cheek.

'Is this *all* the money you received for the land?' Peter asked.

'Oh, yes!' Ananias lied. 'All of it. You can ask my wife!' He looked around, nervously, for Sapphira. What was keeping her? Peter's voice snapped him back to attention.

'I do not need to ask your wife,' said Peter solemnly. 'The Holy Spirit has already told me that what you say is a lie.'

Ananias swallowed hard. Everyone had gone quiet. And all he could hear was Peter's voice and the excited drumming of his own heart.

'Why did you do this wicked thing?' asked Peter. 'The

land was yours. No one forced you to sell it. And after you did, you were free to split up the money any way you liked. So why have you lied to us? And worse still, why have you lied to God?'

Ananias looked round the room. And as he looked, his heart beat faster and faster still. Some faces were confused. Some were angry. But nobody was impressed. Nobody. And then Ananias's heart stopped beating altogether. And he fell to the ground, dead.

Sapphira, meanwhile, had no idea what had happened, no clue that their plan had failed, or that her husband had died. She was still determined to give Ananias plenty of time to work things out. So she fussed with her hair. And ate a meal. And stopped at her neighbour's house for a long gossip. In fact, three hours had passed by the time she got to the meeting place.

Everyone was still there—talking or praying or having a bite to eat. But when Sapphira entered the room, everything went quiet.

'They were obviously more impressed than we imagined!' she thought. But when Sapphira looked more closely at the faces in the room, she realized she was mistaken.

'Sapphira,' Peter called, 'I'd like a word with you.'

This was not looking good. For a moment Sapphira thought about walking out and going back home. But what would Ananias say? And where was her husband, anyway?

'Ananias told us that you sold a piece of land,' Peter explained.

'That's right,' answered Sapphira as confidently as she could.

'And he told us that the land sold for this much.' Here

Peter held up the money bag. 'And that you were giving it all to help the poor.'

Sapphira decided to play it cool. 'Well, that's his money bag,' she chuckled. 'And if that's what he told you, then that must be the case!'

Sapphira looked around. No one was chuckling with her.

Peter just shook his head. 'So you were in this together? Now both of you have lied to God.'

'No, no, no!' Sapphira smiled and tried to explain. 'Not lying. You see, it all depends how you look at it. It all depends on the meaning of the word "got"...'

But before she could finish, Peter spoke again. 'Listen, Sapphira, and listen well. The feet of the men who buried your husband are outside the door. Those men will bury you as well.'

Bury? Husband? Sapphira wondered. But before she could think another thought, she dropped dead to the ground, just like Ananias.

The people certainly were impressed. There was tremendous fear, for a start. And Ananias and Sapphira were the talk of the town for years. Something Sapphira had always wanted.

But what Ananias and Sapphira were remembered for wasn't quite what they'd had in mind!

All Lion books are available from your local
bookshop, or can be ordered via our website
or from Marston Book Services. For a free
catalogue, showing the complete list of titles
available, please contact:

Customer Services
Marston Book Services
PO Box 269
Abingdon
Oxon
OX14 4YN

Tel: 01235 465500
Fax: 01235 465555

Our website can be found at:
www.lion-publishing.co.uk